Bring big smiles to little boys

Fun sweater sets are perfect for playtime, and matching blankets for some sets make them great for naptime, too.

LEISURE ARTS, INC. • Maumelle, Arkansas

Butterfly Set

EASY

SHOPPING LIST

Yarn (Medium Weight)

MEDIUM 4

[3.5 ounces, 170 yards
(100 grams, 156 meters) per skein]:

BLANKET

- ☐ Main Color (Blue) - 6 skeins
- ☐ Contrasting Color (Purple) - 1 skein
- ☐ Color A (Dark Blue) - 1 skein
- ☐ Color B (Aqua) - 1 skein
- ☐ Color C (Lilac) - 1 skein
- ☐ Color D (Pink) - 1 skein
- ☐ Color E (Green) - 1 skein

HAT & CARDIGAN

- ☐ Main Color (Blue) - 2 skeins
- ☐ Contrasting Color (Purple) - 1 skein
- ☐ Color A (Dark Blue) - 1 skein
- ☐ Color B (Aqua) - 1 skein
- ☐ Color C (Lilac) - 1 skein
- ☐ Color D (Pink) - 1 skein
- ☐ Color E (Green) - 1 skein

Crochet Hook

- ☐ Size J (6 mm) **or** size needed for gauge

Additional Supplies

- ☐ Yarn needle
- ☐ Sewing needle and thread
- ☐ ⅝" (16 mm) Buttons (novelty) - {5-6}{6-7-7}

Blanket

Finished Measurement:
39" (99 cm) square

GAUGE INFORMATION

11 sc = 4" (10 cm),
8 sc rows = 2½" (6.25 cm)
One Square (before Edging) = 7" (17.75 cm)
Gauge Swatch: 4" wide x 2½" high (10 cm x 6.25 cm)
Ch 12.
Row 1: Sc in second ch from hook and in each ch across: 11 sc.
Rows 2-8: Ch 1, turn; sc in each sc across.
Finish off.

STITCH GUIDE

TREBLE CROCHET *(abbreviated tr)*
YO twice, insert hook in st indicated, YO and pull up a loop (4 loops on hook), (YO and draw through 2 loops on hook) 3 times.

SQUARE (Make 25)

With Main Color, ch 20.

Row 1 (Right side)**:** Sc in second ch from hook and in each ch across: 19 sc.

Note: Loop a short piece of yarn around any stitch to mark Row 1 as **right** side and bottom edge.

Rows 2-23: Ch 1, turn; sc in each sc across.

Finish off.

EDGING

Work Edging on 5 Squares **each** using Colors A-E.

With **right** side facing, join yarn with sc in first sc on last row ***(see Joining With Sc, page 35)***; 2 sc in same st, sc in each sc across to last sc, 3 sc in last sc; work 17 sc evenly spaced across end of rows; working in free loops of beginning ch ***(Fig. 3, page 35)***, 3 sc in first ch, sc in each ch across to ch at base of last sc, 3 sc in next ch; work 17 sc evenly spaced across end of rows; join with slip st to first sc, finish off: 80 sc.

BUTTERFLY (Make 25)

BODY

With Contrasting Color, ch 14.

Foundation Row (Right side)**:** Sc in second ch from hook and in each ch across to last ch, (sc, ch 2, slip st) in last ch (for head); finish off leaving a long end for sewing: 13 sc.

Note: Mark Foundation Row as **right** side.

WINGS

Make 5 Butterflies **each** in the following five color sequences:

Color Sequence	Rows			
	1	2	Accent	3
#1	A	D	C	E
#2	B	D	E	C
#3	E	C	A	B
#4	C	B	A	D
#5	D	B	E	A

Row 1 - First Side: With **right** side of Body facing, join first color with sc in first sc; ★ skip next 2 sts, tr in next st, (ch 1, tr in same st) 4 times, skip next 2 sts, sc in next st; repeat from ★ once **more**; finish off.

Second Side: With **right** side facing and working in free loops of beginning ch on Body, join first color with sc in same ch as slip st; complete same as First Side.

Row 2 - First Side: With **right** side facing, skip first sc and join next color with sc in first tr; dc in next ch-1 sp, (ch 2, dc in next ch-1 sp) 3 times, sc in next 3 sts, dc in next ch-1 sp, (ch 2, dc in next ch-1 sp) 3 times, sc in next tr, leave last sc unworked; finish off.
Second Side: Work same as First Side.

Accent Row - First Side: With **right** side facing and working in **front** of previous row ***(Fig. A)***, join next color with sc in first unworked tr on Row 1; (ch 3, sc in next tr) twice; finish off. Join same color with sc in first unworked tr of next 5-tr group; (ch 3, sc in next tr) twice; finish off.
Second Side: Work same as First Side.

Fig. A

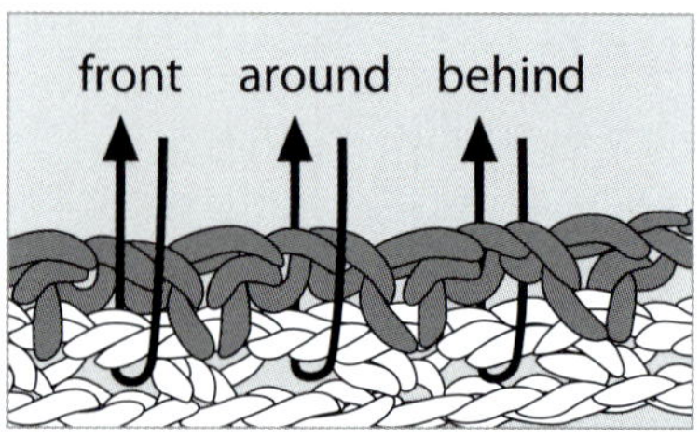

Row 3 - First Side: With **right** side facing, join next color with slip st in first sc on Row 2; sc in same st, † ch 1, working **around** Row 2, sc in first sc on Accent Row, ★ ch 1, sc in next dc on Row 2, ch 1, working **around** Row 2, sc in next sc on Accent Row; repeat from ★ once **more** †, skip next dc on Row 2, slip st in next sc, skip next sc, sc in next sc, repeat from † to † once, ch 1, skip next dc, slip st in last sc; finish off leaving a long end for sewing.
Second Side: Work same as First Side.

ANTENNAE

With Contrasting Color, ch 16; finish off; tie a knot at beginning of chain.

ASSEMBLY

Matching the color of the last row of the Wings to the Edging rnd on a Square, sew the Body of the Butterfly to the center of the Square; do **not** cut yarn.

Weave Antennae through Square behind top of Butterfly Body. Knot remaining end of chain; trim ends. Using long end from Body, tack center of Antennae in place.

Tack Wings in place.

Using Placement Diagram as a guide and Contrasting Color, whipstitch Squares together ***(Fig. 5a, page 36)***, beginning in center sc of one corner 3-sc group and ending in center sc of next corner 3-sc group, forming 5 strips of 5 Squares each; then whipstitch strips together in same manner.

BORDER

Rnd 1: With **right** side of Blanket facing, join Contrasting Color with sc in any sc; sc in each sc and in each joining around working 3 sc in center sc of each corner 3-sc group; join with slip st to first sc, finish off.

Rnd 2: With **right** side facing, join Main Color with sc in any sc; sc in each sc around working 3 sc in center sc of each corner 3-sc group; join with slip st to first sc, finish off.

Rnd 3: With **wrong** side facing and Contrasting Color, repeat Rnd 2.

PLACEMENT DIAGRAM

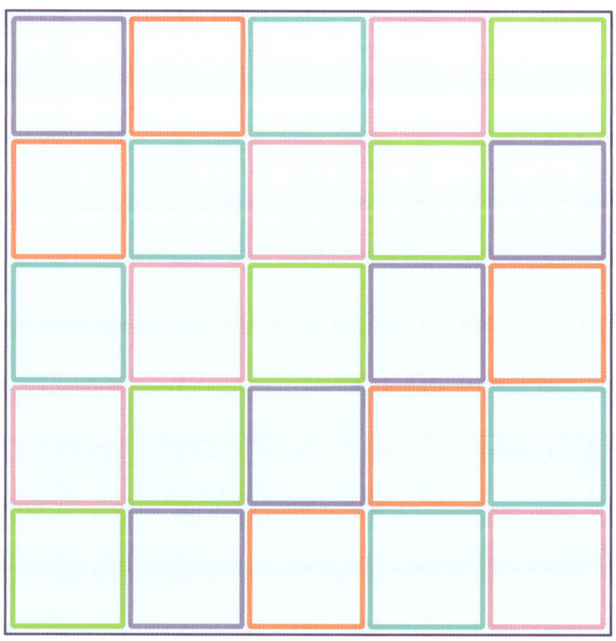

KEY

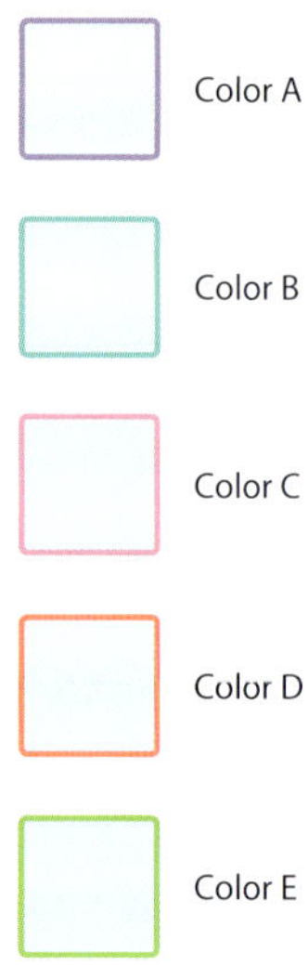

Hat & Cardigan

SIZE INFORMATION

HAT

Size	**Finished Circumference**	
Small	14½"	(37 cm)
Medium	16"	(40.5 cm)
Large	17½"	(44.5 cm)

CARDIGAN

Size	**Finished Chest Measurement**	
6 months	23¾"	(60.5 cm)
1 year	25¾"	(65.5 cm)
2 years	27¼"	(69 cm)
3 years	29½"	(75 cm)
4 years	31¾"	(80.5 cm)

Size Note: We have printed the instructions for the sizes in different colors to make it easier for you to find:

- Size 6 months & small hat in Blue
- Size 1 year in Pink
- Size 2 years & medium hat in Green
- Size 3 years in Orange
- Size 4 years & large hat in Brown

Instructions in Black apply to all sizes.

GAUGE INFORMATION

11 sc = 4" (10 cm),
8 sc rows = 2½" (6.25 cm)

Gauge Swatch: 4" wide x 2½" high (10 cm x 6.25 cm)

Ch 12.

Row 1: Sc in second ch from hook and in each ch across: 11 sc.

Rows 2-8: Ch 1, turn; sc in each sc across.

Finish off.

Hat

STITCH GUIDE

SINGLE CROCHET 2 TOGETHER
(abbreviated sc2tog)
Pull up a loop in each of next 2 sts, YO and draw through all 3 loops on hook (**counts as one sc**).

BODY

With Color A, ch 3; join with slip st to form a ring.

Rnd 1 (Right side)**:** Ch 1, 6 sc in ring; join with slip st to first sc.

Note: Loop a short piece of yarn around any stitch to mark Rnd 1 as **right** side.

Rnd 2: Ch 1, 2 sc in each sc around; cut Color A, with Color B, join with slip st to first sc ***(Fig. 1c, page 35)***: 12 sc.

Rnd 3: Ch 1, sc in same st as joining, 2 sc in next sc, (sc in next sc, 2 sc in next sc) around; join with slip st to first sc: 18 sc.

Rnd 4: Ch 1, sc in same st as joining and in next sc, 2 sc in next sc, (sc in next 2 sc, 2 sc in next sc) around; cut Color B, with Color C, join with slip st to first sc: 24 sc.

Rnd 5: Ch 1, sc in same st as joining and in next 2 sc, 2 sc in next sc, (sc in next 3 sc, 2 sc in next sc) around; join with slip st to first sc: 30 sc.

Rnd 6: Ch 1, sc in same st as joining and in next 3 sc, 2 sc in next sc, (sc in next 4 sc, 2 sc in next sc) around; cut Color C, with Color D, join with slip st to first sc: 36 sc.

Rnd 7: Ch 1, sc in same st as joining and in next 7{4-4} sc, 2 sc in next sc, ★ sc in next 8{5-5} sc, 2 sc in next sc; repeat from ★ around; join with slip st to first sc: 40{42-42} sc.

Size Small Only - Rnd 8: Ch 1, sc in each sc around; cut Color D, with Color E, join with slip st to first sc.

Size Medium Only - Rnd 8: Ch 1, sc in same st as joining and in next 19 sc, 2 sc in next sc, sc in next 20 sc, 2 sc in next sc; cut Color D, with Color E, join with slip st to first sc: 44 sc.

Size Large Only - Rnd 8: Ch 1, sc in same st as joining and in next 5 sc, 2 sc in next sc, (sc in next 6 sc, 2 sc in next sc) around; cut Color D, with Color E, join with slip st to first sc: 48 sc.

ALL SIZES
Rnd 9: Ch 1, sc in each sc around; join with slip st to first sc.

Rnd 10: Ch 1, **turn**; sc in each sc around; cut Color E, with Color A, join with slip st to first sc.

Rnd 11: Ch 1, **turn**; sc in each sc around; join with slip st to first sc.

Size Small Only - Rnds 12-16: Repeat Rnd 11, 5 times working in the following stripe sequence:
1 Rnd Color A, 2 rnds Color B, 2 rnds Color C.

Size Medium Only - Rnds 12-18: Repeat Rnd 11, 7 times working in the following stripe sequence:
1 Rnd Color A, 2 rnds **each** of Color B, Color C, Color D.

Size Large Only - Rnds 12-22: Repeat Rnd 11, 11 times working in the following stripe sequence:
1 Rnd Color A, 2 rnds **each** of Color B, Color C, Color D, Color E, Color A.

All Sizes: Finish off.

FIRST EAR FLAP

Maintain established stripe sequence.

Row 1: With **right** side facing, skip first 3 sc and join next color with sc in next sc ***(see Joining With Sc, page 35)***; sc in next 10{12-14} sc, leave remaining sc unworked: 11{13-15} sc.

Rows 2-4: Ch 1, turn; sc in each sc across.

Row 5 (Decrease row)**:** Ch 1, turn; beginning in first sc, sc2tog, sc in each sc across to last 2 sc, sc2tog: 9{11-13} sc.

Row 6: Ch 1, turn; sc in each sc across.

Rows 7 thru 12{14-16}: Repeat Rows 5 and 6, 3{4-5} times: 3 sc.

Last Row: Ch 1, turn; pull up a loop in first 3 sc, YO and draw through all 4 loops on hook; finish off.

SECOND EAR FLAP

Work in same stripe sequence as First Ear Flap.

Row 1: With **right** side facing, skip next 12 sc from First Ear Flap and join yarn with sc in next sc; sc in next 10{12-14} sc, leave remaining sc unworked: 11{13-15} sc.

Complete same as First Ear Flap.

EDGING

With **right** side facing, join Contrasting Color with sc in first sc on last rnd of Body; sc evenly around entire Hat working (sc, ch 1, sc) in st on last row of each Ear Flap; join with slip st to first sc, finish off.

DECORATIVE TIES

Make 2 chains in each of the following colors: Color A, Color B, and Color D.

Ch 30{35-40}; finish off.

Hold one chain of each color together and insert them through the ch-1 sp at end of the Ear Flap until ends are even. Holding the same color together as one strand, braid the 3 strands; tie end in a knot. Trim the ends.

Repeat for second Ear Flap.

BUTTERFLY (Make 2)

BODY

With Contrasting Color, ch 10.

Foundation Row (Right side)**:** Sc in second ch from hook and in each ch across to last ch, (sc, ch 2, slip st) in last ch (for head); finish off leaving a long end for sewing: 9 sc.

Note: Mark Foundation Row as **right** side.

WINGS

Row 1 - First Side: With **right** side facing, join Color A with sc in first sc; ★ skip next st, dc in next st, (ch 1, dc in same st) twice, skip next st, sc in next st; repeat from ★ once **more**; finish off.

Second Side: With **right** side facing and working in free loops of beginning ch on Body ***(Fig. 3, page 35)***, join Color A with sc in same ch as slip st; complete same as First Side.

Row 2 - First Side: With **right** side facing, skip first sc and join Color C with sc in next dc; (ch 1, skip next st, sc in next dc) 5 times, leave last sc unworked; finish off.

Second Side: Work same as First Side.

Row 3 - First Side: With **right** side facing, join Color D with sc in first unworked sc on Row 1; ch 1, (sc in next ch-1 sp on Row 2, ch 1) twice, working in **front** of previous row ***(Fig. A, page 4)***, sc in skipped sc on Row 1, ch 1, (sc in next ch-1 sp on Row 2, ch 1) twice, sc in last sc on Row 1; finish off.

Second Side: Work same as First Side.

Row 4 - First Side: With **right** side facing, join Color E with sc in same sc as first sc worked into on Row 1, (ch 1, sc in next ch-1 sp on Row 3) 3 times; finish off. Skip next sc, join Color E with sc in next ch-1 sp, ch 1, (sc in next ch-1 sp, ch 1) twice, sc in same sc as last sc worked into on Row 1; finish off.

Second Side: Work same as First Side.

Sew the Body of each Butterfly to the side of the Hat. Tack Wings in place.

ANTENNAE

Insert one strand of Contrasting Color through top of Butterfly Body, tie knot on each end making a 2" (5 cm) length; trim ends.

Cardigan

STITCH GUIDE

DOUBLE TREBLE CROCHET
(abbreviated dtr)
YO 3 times, insert hook in sc indicated, YO and pull up a loop (5 loops on hook), (YO and draw through 2 loops on hook) 4 times.

FRONT POST DOUBLE CROCHET
(abbreviated FPdc)
YO, insert hook from **front** to **back** around post of dc indicated *(Fig. 2, page 35)*, YO and pull up a loop (3 loops on hook), (YO and draw through 2 loops on hook) twice.

BACK POST DOUBLE CROCHET
(abbreviated BPdc)
YO, insert hook from **back** to **front** around post of dc indicated *(Fig. 2, page 35)*, YO and pull up a loop (3 loops on hook), (YO and draw through 2 loops on hook) twice.

SINGLE CROCHET 2 TOGETHER
(abbreviated sc2tog)
Pull up a loop in each of next 2 sc, YO and draw through all 3 loops on hook (**counts as one sc**).

Body is worked in one piece to armholes, then divided for the Fronts and Back.

BODY

With Main Color, ch {62-68}{72-78-84}.

Row 1 (Right side)**:** Sc in second ch from hook and in each ch across: {61-67}{71-77-83} sc.

Note: Loop a short piece of yarn around any stitch to mark Row 1 as **right** side.

Rows 2 thru {16-18}{20-22-24}: Ch 1, turn; sc in each sc across.

RIGHT FRONT

Row 1: Ch 1, turn; sc in first {15-16} {17-19-20} sc, leave remaining sc unworked.

Rows 2 thru {8-10}{12-14-16}: Ch 1, turn; sc in each sc across.

NECK SHAPING

Row 1: Turn; slip st in first {4-4} {5-5-5} sc, ch 1, sc2tog, sc in each sc across: {10-11}{11-13-14} sc.

Rows 2-4: Ch 1, turn; sc in each sc across.

Finish off leaving a long end for sewing.

BACK

Row 1: With **right** side facing, join Main Color with sc in next unworked sc on Body *(see Joining With Sc, page 35)*; sc in next {30-34} {36-38-42} sc, leave remaining sc unworked: {31-35}{37-39-43} sc.

Rows 2 thru {12-14}{16-18-20}: Ch 1, turn; sc in each sc across.

Finish off.

LEFT FRONT

Row 1: With **right** side facing, join Main Color with sc in next unworked sc on Body; sc in each sc across: {15-16}{17-19-20} sc.

Rows 2 thru {8-10}{12-14-16}: Ch 1, turn; sc in each sc across.

NECK SHAPING

Row 1: Ch 1, turn; sc in each sc across to last {6-6}{7-7-7} sc, sc2tog, leave remaining sc unworked: {10-11}{11-13-14} sc.

Rows 2-4: Ch 1, turn; sc in each sc across.

Finish off leaving a long end for sewing.

SLEEVE (Make 2)

With Color A, ch {20-20}{22-22-24}.

Row 1 (Right side)**:** Sc in second ch from hook and in each ch across: {19-19}{21-21-23} sc.

Note: Mark Row 1 as **right** side.

Row 2: Ch 1, turn; sc in each sc across changing to Color B in last sc ***(Fig. 1a, page 35)***.

Work in the following stripe sequence: ★ 2 rows **each** Color B, Color C, Color D, Color E, Color A; repeat from ★ for sequence.

Row 3 (Increase row)**:** Ch 1, turn; 2 sc in first sc, sc in each sc across to last sc, 2 sc in last sc: {21-21}{23-23-25} sc.

Row 4: Ch 1, turn; sc in each sc across changing to next color in last sc.

Rows 5 thru {6-8}{8-12-14}: Repeat Rows 3 and 4, {1-2}{2-4-5} time(s): {23-25}{27-31-35} sc.

Work even for {10-12}{14-14-14} rows.

Finish off.

SLEEVE RIBBING

Row 1: With **right** side facing and working in free loops of beginning ch ***(Fig. 3, page 35)***, join Contrasting Color with dc in first ch ***(see Joining With Dc, page 35)***; dc in next ch and in each ch across: {19-19}{21-21-23} dc.

Row 2: Ch 2, turn; skip first dc, (work BPdc around next dc, work FPdc around next dc) across; finish off.

FINISHING

With **wrong** sides together, whipstitch shoulder seams ***(Fig. 5a, page 36)***.

Sew Sleeves to armholes, matching center of Sleeves to shoulder seams. Whipstitch underarm seam ***(Fig. 5b, page 36)***.

BOTTOM RIBBING

Row 1: With **right** side facing and working in free loops of beginning ch, join Contrasting Color with dc in first ch; dc in next ch and in each ch across: {61-67}{71-77-83} dc.

Row 2: Ch 2, turn; skip first dc, (work BPdc around next dc, work FPdc around next dc) across; finish off.

NECK RIBBING

Row 1: With **right** side facing, join Contrasting Color with dc in first unworked st at Right Front neck edge; dc in next {3-3}{4-4-4} sts, work 7 dc evenly spaced across end of rows, dc in next {11-13}{15-13-15} sc across Back, work 7 dc evenly spaced across end of rows, dc in next {4-4}{5-5-5} sc: {33-35}{39-37-39} dc.

Row 2: Ch 2, turn; skip first dc, (work BPdc around next dc, work FPdc around next dc) across; finish off.

BUTTON BAND

The Button Band is made on the Left Front for Girl's cardigan and on the Right Front for Boy's cardigan.

Row 1: With **right** side facing, join Contrasting Color with sc in end of first row on Ribbing; work {24-29}{29-34-40} sc evenly spaced across Front edge: {25-30}{30-35-41} sc.

Row 2: Ch 1, turn; sc in Front Loop Only of each sc across ***(Fig. B)***.

Fig. B

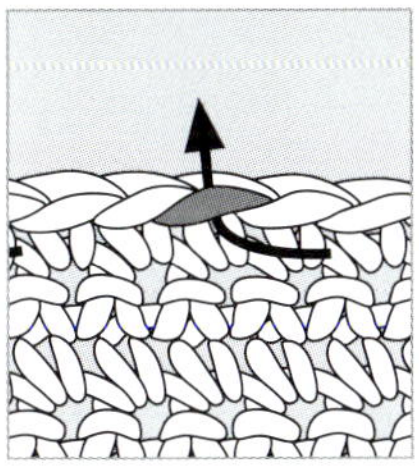

Rows 3-5: Ch 1, turn; sc in both loops of each sc across.

Finish off.

BUTTONHOLE BAND

Row 1: With **right** side of remaining Front edge facing, join Contrasting Color with sc in end of first row on Ribbing; work {24-29}{29-34-40} sc evenly spaced across Front edge: {25-30}{30-35-41} sc.

Row 2: Ch 1, turn; sc in Front Loop Only of each sc across.

Row 3 (Buttonhole row)**:** Ch 1, turn; working in both loops, sc in first 2 sc, ★ ch 1, skip next sc (**buttonhole made**), sc in next {4-4}{4-4-5} sc; repeat from ★ across to last 3 sc, ch 1, skip next sc, sc in last 2 sc: {5-6}{6-7-7} ch-1 sps.

Row 4: Ch 1, turn; sc in each sc and in each ch-1 sp across: {25-30} {30-35-41} sc.

Row 5: Ch 1, turn; sc in each sc across; finish off.

Sew buttons to Button Band matching buttonholes.

BUTTERFLY WINGS

LEFT FRONT

Row 1: With **right** side facing and working in free loops of sc on Row 1 of Band ***(Fig. C)***, skip first {2-5} {5-7-10} sc and join Color A with sc in next sc; ★ skip next 4 sc, dtr in next sc, (ch 1, dtr in same st) 6 times, skip next 4 sc, sc in next sc; repeat from ★ once **more**, leave remaining sc unworked; finish off: 3 sc and 12 ch-1 sps.

Fig. C

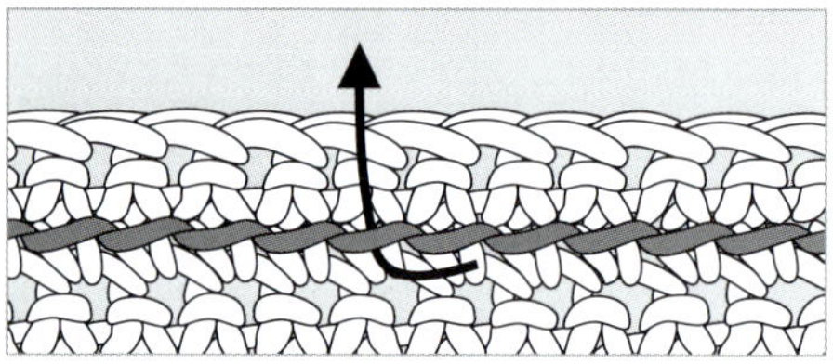

Row 2: With **right** side facing, join Color B with sc in first sc; ★ † dc in next ch-1 sp, (ch 1, dc in same sp) twice, sc in next ch-1 sp †; repeat from † to † 2 times **more**, skip next dtr, sc in next sc; repeat from ★ once **more**; finish off.

Row 3: † With **right** side facing, join Color C with sc in center dc of first 3-dc group; † ★ skip next dc, dc in next sc, (ch 2, dc in same st) twice, skip next dc, sc in next dc; repeat from ★ once **more**; finish off †. With **right** side facing, join Color C with sc in center dc of next 3-dc group; repeat from † to † once.

Row 4: With **right** side facing, join Color D with sc in first sc on Row 1 (already worked into); sc in first sc on Row 2 and in next dc and ch-1 sp, † sc in first sc on Row 3 and in each st and ch-2 sp across Row 3, sc in same dc as last sc on Row 3 is worked into, sc in next ch-1 sp on Row 2 †, sc in next 4 sts and in next ch-1 sp, sc in next dc (already worked into), repeat from † to † once, sc in last 3 sts and in last dtr on Row 1; finish off: 44 sc.

Row 5: With **right** side facing, join Color E with sc in first sc on Row 4; † sc in next sc, ★ ch 2, slip st in second ch from hook, skip next sc, sc in next 2 sc; repeat from ★ 5 times **more** †, slip st in next sc; finish off. Skip next 4 sc and join Color E with sc in next sc; repeat from † to † once, ch 2, slip st in second ch from hook, skip next sc, slip st in last sc; finish off.

RIGHT FRONT

Row 1: With **right** side facing and working in free loops of sc on Row 1 of Band, skip first {2-4}{4-7-10} sc and join Color A with sc in next sc; ★ skip next 4 sc, dtr in next sc, (ch 1, dtr in same st) 6 times, skip next 4 sc, sc in next sc; repeat from ★ once **more**, leave remaining sc unworked; finish off: 3 sc and 12 ch-1 sps.

Rows 2-5: Work same as Left Front.

Overlap top Wing over bottom Wing and tack Wings in place.

Star-Struck Set

EASY

Hat & Cardigan

SHOPPING LIST

Yarn (Medium Weight) MEDIUM 4

[3.5 ounces, 170 yards (100 grams, 156 meters) per skein]:

- ☐ Color A (Black) - {1-1}{1-1-2} skein(s)
- ☐ Color B (Navy) - 1 skein
- ☐ Color C (Blue) - 1 skein
- ☐ Color D (Dark Grey) - 1 skein

[3 ounces, 185 yards (85 grams, 170 meters) per skein]:

- ☐ Color E (Grey) - 1 skein

Crochet Hook

- ☐ Size J (6 mm) **or** size needed for gauge

Additional Supplies

- ☐ Yarn needle
- ☐ Sewing needle and thread
- ☐ ⅝" (16 mm) Buttons (novelty) - {5-6}{6-7-7}

SIZE INFORMATION

HAT

Size	Finished Circumference	
Small	14½"	(37 cm)
Medium	16"	(40.5 cm)
Large	17½"	(44.5 cm)

CARDIGAN

Size	Finished Chest Measurement	
6 months	23¾"	(60.5 cm)
1 year	25¾"	(65.5 cm)
2 years	27¼"	(69 cm)
3 years	29½"	(75 cm)
4 years	31¾"	(80.5 cm)

Size Note: We have printed the instructions for the sizes in different colors to make it easier for you to find:

- Size 6 months & small hat in Blue
- Size 1 year in Pink
- Size 2 years & medium hat in Green
- Size 3 years in Orange
- Size 4 years & large hat in Brown

Instructions in Black apply to all sizes.

GAUGE INFORMATION

11 sc = 4" (10 cm), 8 sc rows = 2½" (6.25 cm)

Gauge Swatch: 4" wide x 2½" high (10 cm x 6.25 cm)

Ch 12.

Row 1: Sc in second ch from hook and in each ch across: 11 sc.

Rows 2-8: Ch 1, turn; sc in each sc across.

Finish off.

STITCH GUIDE

FRONT POST DOUBLE CROCHET
(abbreviated FPdc)
YO, insert hook from **front** to **back** around post of dc indicated *(Fig. 2, page 35)*, YO and pull up a loop (3 loops on hook), (YO and draw through 2 loops on hook) twice.

BACK POST DOUBLE CROCHET
(abbreviated BPdc)
YO, insert hook from **back** to **front** around post of dc indicated *(Fig. 2, page 35)*, YO and pull up a loop (3 loops on hook), (YO and draw through 2 loops on hook) twice.

SINGLE CROCHET 2 TOGETHER
(abbreviated sc2tog)
Pull up a loop in each of next 2 sc, YO and draw through all 3 loops on hook (**counts as one sc**).

HAT

BODY

With Color C, ch 40{44-48}; being careful **not** to twist ch, join with slip st to form a ring.

Rnd 1 (Right side)**:** Ch 1, sc in same ch as joining and in each ch around; join with slip st to first sc: 40{44-48} sc.

Note: Loop a short piece of yarn around any stitch to mark Rnd 1 as **right** side.

Rnd 2: Ch 1, turn; sc in each sc around; cut Color C, with Color D, join with slip st to first sc *(Fig. 1c, page 35)*.

Work in the following stripe sequence: ★ 2 rnds **each** Color D, Color E, Color B, Color C; repeat from ★ for sequence.

Rnd 3: Ch 1, turn; sc in each sc around; join with slip st to first sc.

Rnd 4: Ch 1, turn; sc in each sc around; cut yarn, with next color, join with slip st to first sc.

Rnds 5 thru 14{16-18}: Repeat Rnds 3 and 4, 5{6-7} times working in the stripe sequence.

SHAPING

Continue working in the established stripe sequence.

Rnd 1: Ch 1, turn; sc in same sc as joining and in next sc, sc2tog, (sc in next 2 sc, sc2tog) around; join with slip st to first sc: 30{33-36} sc.

Rnd 2: Ch 1, turn; sc in each sc around; join with slip st to first sc.

Rnd 3: Ch 1, turn; sc in same sc as joining, sc2tog, (sc in next sc, sc2tog) around; join with slip st to first sc: 20{22-24} sc.

Rnd 4: Repeat Rnd 2.

Rnd 5: Ch 1, turn; beginning in same sc as joining, sc2tog around; join with slip st to first sc: 10{11-12} sc.

Rnd 6: Repeat Rnd 2.

Rnd 7: Ch 1, turn; beginning in same sc as joining, sc2tog around to last 0{1-0} sc, sc in last 0{1-0} sc *(see Zeros, page 35)*; join with slip st to first sc, finish off leaving a long end for sewing: 5{6-6} sc.

Weave yarn end through sts on Rnd 7 to close *(Fig. 4, page 35)*; secure yarn.

BRIM

Rnd 1: With **right** side facing and working in free loops of beginning ch ***(Fig. 3, page 35)***, join Color B with dc in first ch ***(see Joining With Dc, page 35)***, dc in next ch and in each ch around; join with slip st to first dc: 40{44-48} dc.

Rnd 2: Ch 2, turn; work FPdc around next dc, (work BPdc around next dc, work FPdc around next dc) around; join with slip st to first st, finish off.

EAR FLAP (Make 2)

With Color B, ch 12{14-16}.

Row 1 (Right side)**:** Sc in second ch from hook and in each ch across: 11{13-15} sc.

Note: Mark Row 1 as **right** side.

Rows 2-4: Ch 1, turn; sc in each sc across.

Row 5 (Decrease row)**:** Ch 1, turn; beginning in first sc, sc2tog, sc in each sc across to last 2 sc, sc2tog: 9{11-13} sc.

Row 6: Ch 1, turn; sc in each sc across.

Rows 7 thru 12{14-16}: Repeat Rows 5 and 6, 3{4-5} times: 3 sc.

Finish off.

Edging: With **right** side facing and working in end of rows, join Color B with sc in first row ***(see Joining With Sc, page 35)***; sc in each row across, (sc, ch 1, sc) in sc on last row, sc in each row across; finish off leaving a long end for sewing.

SMALL STAR (Make 2)

With Color E, ch 3; join with slip st to form a ring.

Rnd 1: Ch 1, 5 sc in ring; join with slip st to first sc.

Rnd 2: ★ Ch 3, slip st in second ch from hook, sc in next ch, slip st in next sc; repeat from ★ around working last slip st in joining slip st; finish off leaving a long end for sewing.

Sew a Star to **right** side of each Ear Flap.

Sew Ear Flaps to beginning ch of Body, placing them behind the Brim with edge of both Ear Flaps together at the joining on the Body.

DECORATIVE TIES

Make 2 chains in each of the following colors: Color B, Color C, and Color D.

Ch 30{35-40}; finish off.

Hold one chain of each color together and insert them through ch-1 sp at end of the Ear Flap until ends are even. Holding the same color together as one strand, braid the 3 strands; tie end in a knot. Trim the ends.

Repeat for second Ear Flap.

LARGE STAR (Make 4)

With Color E, ch 4; join with slip st to form a ring.

Rnd 1: Ch 1, 10 sc in ring; join with slip st to first sc.

Rnd 2: ★ Ch 4, slip st in second ch from hook, sc in next ch, hdc in next ch, skip next sc, slip st in next sc; repeat from ★ around working last slip st in joining slip st; finish off.

Chain: Join Color B with slip st in point of Large Star; ch 12{14-16}; finish off leaving a long end for sewing.

Sew end of each chain to top of hat.

CARDIGAN

Body is worked in one piece to armholes, then divided for the Fronts and Back.

BODY

With Color C, ch {62-68}{72-78-84}.

Row 1 (Right side)**:** Sc in second ch from hook and in each ch across: {61-67}{71-77-83} sc.

Note: Loop a short piece of yarn around any stitch to mark Row 1 as **right** side.

Row 2: Ch 1, turn; sc in each sc across changing to Color D in last sc ***(Fig. 1a, page 35)***; cut Color C.

Work in the following stripe sequence: ★ 2 rows **each** Color D, Color E, Color A, Color C; repeat from ★ for sequence.

Row 3: Ch 1, turn; sc in each sc across.

Row 4: Ch 1, turn; sc in each sc across changing to next color in last sc.

Rows 5 thru {16-18}{20-22-24}: Repeat Rows 3 and 4, {6-7}{8-9-10} times working in the established stripe sequence.

RIGHT FRONT

Continue working in the established stripe sequence throughout.

Row 1: Ch 1, turn; sc in first {15-16}{17-19-20} sc, leave remaining sc unworked.

Rows 2 thru {8-10}{12-14-16}: Ch 1, turn; sc in each sc across.

NECK SHAPING

Row 1: Turn; slip st in first {4-4} {5-5-5} sc, ch 1, sc2tog, sc in each sc across: {10-11}{11-13-14} sc.

Rows 2-4: Ch 1, turn; sc in each sc across.

Finish off leaving a long end for sewing.

BACK

Row 1: With **right** side facing, join next color with sc in next unworked sc on Body ***(see Joining With Sc, page 35)***; sc in next {30-34} {36-38-42} sc, leave remaining sc unworked: {31-35}{37-39-43} sc.

Rows 2 thru {12-14}{16-18-20}: Ch 1, turn; sc in each sc across.

Finish off.

LEFT FRONT

Row 1: With **right** side facing, join next color with sc in next unworked sc on Body; sc in each sc across: {15-16}{17-19-20} sc.

Rows 2 thru {8-10}{12-14-16}: Ch 1, turn; sc in each sc across.

NECK SHAPING

Row 1: Ch 1, turn; sc in each sc across to last {6-6}{7-7-7} sc, sc2tog, leave remaining sc unworked: {10-11} {11-13-14} sc.

Rows 2-4: Ch 1, turn; sc in each sc across.

Finish off leaving a long end for sewing.

SLEEVE (Make 2)

With Color C, ch {20-20}{22-22-24}.

Row 1 (Right side)**:** Sc in second ch from hook and in each ch across: {19-19}{21-21-23} sc.

Note: Mark Row 1 as **right** side.

Row 2: Ch 1, turn; sc in each sc across changing to Color D in last sc.

Work in the following stripe sequence: ★ 2 rows **each** Color D, Color E, Color A, Color C; repeat from ★ for sequence.

Row 3 (Increase row)**:** Ch 1, turn; 2 sc in first sc, sc in each sc across to last sc, 2 sc in last sc: {21-21}{23-23-25} sc.

Row 4: Ch 1, turn; sc in each sc across changing to next color in last sc.

Rows 5 thru {6-8}{8-12-14}: Repeat Rows 3 and 4, {1-2}{2-4-5} time(s): {23-25}{27-31-33} sc.

Work even for {10-12}{14-14-14} rows.

Finish off.

SLEEVE RIBBING

Row 1: With **right** side facing and working in free loops of beginning ch ***(Fig. 3, page 35)***, join Color A with dc in first ch ***(see Joining With Dc, page 35)***; dc in next ch and in each ch across: {19-19}{21-21-23} dc.

Row 2: Ch 2, turn; skip first dc, (work BPdc around next dc, work FPdc around next dc) across; finish off.

FINISHING

With **wrong** sides together, whipstitch shoulder seams ***(Fig. 5a, page 36)***.

Sew Sleeves to armholes, matching center of Sleeves to shoulder seams. Whipstitch underarm seam ***(Fig. 5b, page 36)***.

BOTTOM RIBBING

Row 1: With **right** side facing and working in free loops of beginning ch, join Color A with dc in first ch; dc in next ch and in each ch across: {61-67}{71-77-83} dc.

Row 2: Ch 2, turn; skip first dc, (work BPdc around next dc, work FPdc around next dc) across; finish off.

NECK RIBBING

Row 1: With **right** side facing, join Color A with dc in first unworked st at Right Front neck edge; dc in next {3-3}{4-4-4} sts, work 7 dc evenly spaced across end of rows, dc in next {11-13}{15-13-15} sc across Back, work 7 dc evenly spaced across end of rows, dc in next {4-4}{5-5-5} sc: {33-35}{39-37-39} dc.

Row 2: Ch 2, turn; skip first dc, (work BPdc around next dc, work FPdc around next dc) across; finish off.

BUTTON BAND

The Button Band is made on the Left Front for Girl's cardigan and on the Right Front for Boy's cardigan.

Row 1: With **right** side facing, join Color A with sc in end of first row on Ribbing; work {24-29}{29-34-40} sc evenly spaced across Front edge: {25-30}{30-35-41} sc.

Rows 2-5: Ch 1, turn; sc in each sc across.

Finish off.

BUTTONHOLE BAND

Row 1: With **right** side of remaining Front edge facing, join Color A with sc in end of first row on Ribbing; work {24-29}{29-34-40} sc evenly spaced across Front edge: {25-30}{30-35-41} sc.

Row 2: Ch 1, turn; sc in each sc across.

Row 3 (Buttonhole row)**:** Ch 1, turn; sc in first 2 sc, ★ ch 1, skip next sc **(buttonhole made)**, sc in next {4-4}{4-4-5} sc; repeat from ★ across to last 3 sc, ch 1, skip next sc, sc in last 2 sc: {5-6}{6-7-7} ch-1 sps.

Row 4: Ch 1, turn; sc in each sc and in each ch-1 sp across: {25-30}{30-35-41} sc.

Row 5: Ch 1, turn; sc in each sc across; finish off.

Sew buttons to Button Band matching buttonholes.

STAR

With Color E, ch 3; join with slip st to form a ring.

Rnd 1: Ch 1, 8 sc in ring; join with slip st to first sc.

Rnd 2: Ch 1, sc in same sc as joining, 2 sc in each of next 7 sc; join with slip st to first sc: 15 sc.

Rnd 3: ★ Ch 4, sc in second ch from hook, hdc in next ch, dc in next ch, skip next sc, slip st in next 2 sc; repeat from ★ around working last slip st in joining slip st; finish off leaving a long end for sewing.

Using photo, page 14, as a guide for placement, sew Star on Left Front.

Hoodie

SHOPPING LIST

Yarn (Medium Weight) MEDIUM 4

[3.5 ounces, 170 yards
(100 grams, 156 meters) per skein]:

- ☐ Main Color (Dark Grey) - {3-3}{3-3-4} skeins
- ☐ Color A (Navy) - {1-1}{1-2-2} skein(s)
- ☐ Color B (Blue) - 1 skein

[3 ounces, 185 yards
(85 grams, 170 meters) per skein]:

- ☐ Color C (Grey) - 1 skein

Crochet Hooks

- ☐ Size L (8 mm)
  or size needed for gauge
- ☐ Size K (6.5 mm) for Star

Additional Supplies

- ☐ Yarn needle
- ☐ Sewing needle and thread
- ☐ Zipper - {18-18}{20-22-24}"/
  {45.5-45.5}{51-56-61} cm length

SIZE INFORMATION

Size	Finished Chest Measurement	
6 months	23½"	(59.5 cm)
1 year	25½"	(65 cm)
2 years	27½"	(70 cm)
3 years	29½"	(75 cm)
4 years	31½"	(80 cm)

Size Note: We have printed the instructions for the sizes in different colors to make it easier for you to find:

- Size 6 months in Blue
- Size 1 year in Pink
- Size 2 years in Green
- Size 3 years in Orange
- Size 4 years in Brown

Instructions in Black apply to all sizes.

The Pullover is made holding two strands together as one throughout. The Star only uses one strand.

GAUGE INFORMATION

Holding 2 strands together, 8 sts = 4" (10 cm),
6 dc rows = 5" (12.75 cm), 6 sc rows = 2½" (6.25 cm)

Gauge Swatch: 4" wide x 5" high (10 cm x 12.75 cm)

With larger size hook and holding 2 strands of Main Color together, ch 10.

Row 1: Dc in fourth ch from hook **(3 skipped chs count as first dc)** and in each ch across: 8 dc.

Rows 2-6: Ch 3 **(counts as first dc)**, turn; dc in next dc and in each dc across.

Finish off.

STITCH GUIDE

FRONT POST DOUBLE CROCHET ***(abbreviated FPdc)***

YO, insert hook from **front** to **back** around post of dc indicated ***(Fig. 2, page 35)***, YO and pull up a loop (3 loops on hook), (YO and draw through 2 loops on hook) twice.

BACK POST DOUBLE CROCHET ***(abbreviated BPdc)***

YO, insert hook from **back** to **front** around post of dc indicated ***(Fig. 2, page 35)***, YO and pull up a loop (3 loops on hook), (YO and draw through 2 loops on hook) twice.

SINGLE CROCHET 2 TOGETHER ***(abbreviated sc2tog)***

Pull up a loop in each of next 2 sc, YO and draw through all 3 loops on hook **(counts as one sc)**.

FRONT

With larger size hook and holding 2 strands of Main Color together, ch {24-26}{28-30-32}.

Row 1 (Right side)**:** Dc in fourth ch from hook **(3 skipped chs count as first dc, now and throughout)** and in each ch across: {22-24}{26-28-30} dc.

Note: Loop a short piece of yarn around any stitch to mark Row 1 as **right** side.

Rows 2 thru {9-10}{11-12-13}: Ch 3 **(counts as first dc, now and throughout)**, turn; dc in next dc and in each dc across.

First Shoulder: Ch 3, turn; dc in next {5-6}{7-8-9} dc, leave remaining dc unworked; finish off leaving a long end for sewing: {6-7}{8-9-10} dc.

Second Shoulder: Skip next 10 dc from First Shoulder and join Main Color with dc in next dc ***(see Joining With Dc, page 35)***; dc in last {5-6}{7-8-9} dc; finish off leaving a long end for sewing: {6-7}{8-9-10} dc.

BACK (Make 2)

With larger size hook and holding 2 strands of Main Color together, ch {13-14}{15-16-17}.

Row 1 (Right side)**:** Dc in fourth ch from hook and in each ch across: {11-12}{13-14-15} dc.

Note: Mark Row 1 as **right** side.

Rows 2 thru {10-11}{12-13-14}: Ch 3, turn; dc in next dc and in each dc across.

Finish off.

SLEEVE (Make 2)

With larger size hook and holding 2 strands of Color B together, ch {15-15}{16-16-17}.

Row 1 (Right side)**:** Sc in second ch from hook and in each ch across: {14-14}{15-15-16} sc.

Note: Mark Row 1 as **right** side.

Row 2: Ch 1, turn; sc in each sc across changing to Main Color in last sc ***(Fig. 1a, page 35)***; cut Color B.

Work in the following stripe sequence: ★ 2 rows **each** Main Color, Color C, Color A, Color B; repeat from ★ for sequence.

Row 3 (Increase row)**:** Ch 1, turn; 2 sc in first sc, sc in each sc across to last sc, 2 sc in last sc: {16-16}{17-17-18} sc.

Row 4: Ch 1, turn; sc in each sc across changing to next color in last sc.

Rows 5 thru {8-10}{12-12-16}: Repeat Rows 3 and 4, {2-3}{4-4-6} times: {20-22}{25-25-30} sc.

Work even for {2-2}{2-4-2} rows.

Finish off.

SLEEVE RIBBING

Row 1: With **right** side facing and working in free loops of beginning ch ***(Fig. 3, page 35)***, using larger size hook and holding two strands of Color A together, join yarn with dc in first ch; dc in next ch and in each ch across: {14-14}{15-15-16} dc.

Row 2: Ch 2, turn; skip first dc, work FPdc around next dc, (work BPdc around next dc, work FPdc around next dc) across; finish off.

HOOD

With larger size hook and holding 2 strands of Main Color together, ch {32-36}{38-42-44}.

Row 1 (Right side)**:** Dc in fourth ch from hook and in each ch across: {30-34}{36-40-42} dc.

Note: Mark Row 1 as **right** side.

Rows 2 thru {6-7}{8-9-10}: Ch 3, turn; dc in next dc and in each dc across.

Finish off.

HOOD RIBBING

Row 1: With **right** side facing and working in free loops of beginning ch, using larger size hook and holding two strands of Color A together, join yarn with dc in first ch; dc in next ch and in each ch across: {30-34}{36-40-42} dc.

Row 2: Ch 2, turn; skip first dc, work FPdc around next dc, (work BPdc around next dc, work FPdc around next dc) across; finish off.

FINISHING

STAR

With smaller size hook and one strand of Color C, ch 4; join with slip st to form a ring.

Rnd 1 (Right side)**:** Ch 3, 14 dc in ring; join with slip st to first dc: 15 dc.

Note: Mark Rnd 1 as **right** side.

Rnd 2: Ch 3, dc in same dc as joining, 2 dc in next dc and in each dc around; join with slip st to first dc: 30 dc.

Rnd 3: Ch 3, 2 dc in next dc, (dc in next dc, 2 dc in next dc) around; join with slip st to first dc: 45 dc.

FIRST POINT

Row 1: Ch 1, sc in next 9 dc, leave remaining dc unworked.

Rows 2-4: Ch 1, turn; beginning in first sc, sc2tog, sc in each sc across to last 2 sc, sc2tog: 3 sc.

Row 5: Ch 1, turn; pull up a loop in each of first 3 sc, YO and draw through all 4 loops on hook; finish off.

NEXT 4 POINTS

Row 1: With **right** side facing, join Color C with sc in next unworked dc on Rnd 3; sc in next 8 dc: 9 sc.

Rows 2-5: Work same as First Point.

Using photo as a guide for placement, sew Star on Front, sewing along the edge of the Star and also within the Star.

With **wrong** sides together, whipstitch shoulder seams ***(Fig. 5a, page 36)***.

Sew Sleeves to Body, matching center of Sleeves to shoulder seam and beginning {5-5½}{6¼-6¼-7½}"/{12.5-14}{16-16-19} cm down from seam.

Whipstitch underarm and side in one continuous seam ***(Fig. 5b, page 36)***.

BOTTOM RIBBING

Row 1: With **right** side facing and working in free loops of beginning ch, using larger size hook and holding two strands of Color A together, join yarn with dc in first ch; dc in next ch and in each ch across: {44-48}{52-56-60} dc.

Row 2: Ch 2, turn; skip first dc, work FPdc around next dc, (work BPdc around next dc, work FPdc around next dc) across; finish off.

BACK EDGING

Row 1: With **right** side facing and working in end of rows, using larger size hook and holding two strands of Color A together, join yarn with sc in first row on Back Ribbing; sc evenly across; with **right** side of Hood facing, sc in each dc across last row; sc evenly across end of rows on Back.

Row 2: Ch 1, turn; sc in each sc across; finish off.

Placing each end of Row 2 of Hood Edging together at center Front, sew end of rows to Body.

Sew zipper in place to Back opening.

Ladybug & Bumblebee Set

Blanket

EASY

Finished Measurement:
37" (94 cm) square

SHOPPING LIST

Yarn (Medium Weight) MEDIUM 4

[3.5 ounces, 170 yards
(100 grams, 156 meters) per skein]:

- ☐ Black - 3 skeins
- ☐ Red - 3 skeins
- ☐ Yellow - 2 skeins

Crochet Hook

- ☐ Size J (6 mm)
  or size needed for gauge

GAUGE INFORMATION

11 dc = 4" (10 cm),
4 dc rows = 2½" (6.25 cm)

Gauge Swatch: 4" wide x 2½" high (10 cm x 6.25 cm)

Ch 13.

Row 1: Dc in fourth ch from hook **(3 skipped chs count as first dc)** and in each ch across: 11 dc.

Rows 2-4: Ch 3 **(counts as first dc)**, turn; dc in next dc and in each dc across.

Finish off.

STITCH GUIDE

CLUSTER (uses one st)

★ With Black, YO, insert hook in st indicated, YO and pull up a loop, YO and draw through 2 loops on hook; repeat from ★ 3 times **more**, drop Black, with Red, YO and draw through all 5 loops on hook. Push Cluster to **right** side. Carry Black across **wrong** side and cut yarn after last Cluster in row is made.

BODY

With Red, ch 101.

Row 1 (Right side)**:** Dc in fourth ch from hook **(3 skipped chs count as first dc)** and in each ch across: 99 dc.

Note: Loop a short piece of yarn around any stitch to mark Row 1 as **right** side.

Row 2: Ch 3 **(counts as first dc, now and throughout)**, turn; dc in next 3 dc changing to Black in last dc made ***(Fig. 1b, page 35)***, work Cluster in next dc, ★ dc in next 5 dc changing to Black in last dc made, work Cluster in next dc; repeat from ★ across to last 4 dc, dc in last 4 dc: 16 Clusters and 83 dc.

Work over Black strands to hide yarn.

Row 3: Ch 3, turn; dc in next dc and in each st across: 99 dc.

Row 4: Ch 2, drop Red, with Black, ch 1, turn; work Cluster in next dc, ★ dc in next 5 dc changing to Black in last dc made, work Cluster in next dc; repeat from ★ across to last dc, dc in last dc: 17 Clusters and 82 dc.

Row 5: Ch 3, turn; dc in next st and in each st across: 99 dc.

Rows 6-11: Repeat Rows 2-5 once, then repeat Rows 2 and 3 once **more**; at end of Row 11, finish off.

Row 12: With **right** side facing, join Black with sc in first dc ***(see Joining With Sc, page 35)***; sc in each dc across.

Row 13: Ch 1, turn; sc in each sc across changing to Yellow in last sc ***(Fig. 1a, page 35)***; do **not** cut Black.

Carry unused yarn along edge.

Row 14: Ch 3, turn; dc in next st and in each st across.

Rows 15-23: Repeat Row 14, working in the following color sequence: 1 Row Yellow, (2 rows Black, 2 rows Yellow) twice; at end of Row 23, change to Black in last dc and cut Yellow.

Rows 24 and 25: Ch 1, turn; sc in each st across; at end of Row 25, change to Red in last sc; cut Black.

Row 26: Ch 3, turn; dc in next sc and in each sc across.

Rows 27-63: Repeat Rows 2-26 once, then repeat Rows 2-13 once **more**; at end of Row 63, do **not** change colors or finish off.

EDGING

Rnd 1: Ch 1, turn; 3 sc in first sc, sc in each sc across to last sc, 3 sc in last sc; sc evenly across end of rows; working in free loops of beginning ch ***(Fig. 3, page 35)***, 3 sc in first ch, sc in each ch across to last ch, 3 sc in last ch; sc evenly across end of rows; join with slip st to first sc.

Rnd 2: Ch 1, **turn**; sc in each sc around working 3 sc in center sc of each corner 3-sc group; join with slip st to first sc, finish off.

Ladybug Hat & Cardigan

SHOPPING LIST

Yarn (Medium Weight) 4

[3.5 ounces, 170 yards (100 grams, 156 meters) per skein]:

- ☐ Red - {2-2}{2-3-3} skeins
- ☐ Black - {1-1}{2-2-2} skein(s)

Crochet Hook

- ☐ Size J (6 mm) **or** size needed for gauge

Additional Supplies

- ☐ Yarn needle
- ☐ Sewing needle and thread
- ☐ ⅝" (16 mm) Buttons (novelty) - {6-6}{7-8-8}

SIZE INFORMATION

HAT

Size	**Finished Circumference**	
Small	15¼"	(38.5 cm)
Medium	16¼"	(41.5 cm)
Large	17½"	(44.5 cm)

CARDIGAN

Size	**Finished Chest Measurement**	
6 months	23¾"	(60.5 cm)
1 year	25¾"	(65.5 cm)
2 years	27¼"	(69 cm)
3 years	29½"	(75 cm)
4 years	31¾"	(80.5 cm)

Size Note: We have printed the instructions for the sizes in different colors to make it easier for you to find:

- Size 6 months & small hat in Blue
- Size 1 year in Pink
- Size 2 years & medium hat in Green
- Size 3 years in Orange
- Size 4 years & large hat in Brown

Instructions in Black apply to all sizes.

GAUGE INFORMATION

11 dc = 4" (10 cm),
4 dc rows = 2½" (6.25 cm)

Gauge Swatch: 4" wide x 2½" high (10 cm x 6.25 cm)

Ch 13.

Row 1: Dc in fourth ch from hook **(3 skipped chs count as first dc)** and in each ch across: 11 dc.

Rows 2-4: Ch 3 **(counts as first dc)**, turn; dc in next dc and in each dc across.

Finish off.

STITCH GUIDE

FRONT POST DOUBLE CROCHET ***(abbreviated FPdc)***

YO, insert hook from **front** to **back** around post of dc indicated ***(Fig. 2, page 35)***, YO and pull up a loop (3 loops on hook), (YO and draw through 2 loops on hook) twice.

BACK POST DOUBLE CROCHET ***(abbreviated BPdc)***

YO, insert hook from **back** to **front** around post of dc indicated ***(Fig. 2, page 35)***, YO and pull up a loop (3 loops on hook), (YO and draw through 2 loops on hook) twice.

CLUSTER (uses one st)

★ With Black, YO, insert hook in st indicated, YO and pull up a loop, YO and draw through 2 loops on hook; repeat from ★ 3 times **more**, drop Black, with Red, YO and draw through all 5 loops on hook. Push Cluster to **right** side. Carry Black across **wrong** side and cut yarn after last Cluster in row/round is made.

SINGLE CROCHET 2 TOGETHER ***(abbreviated sc2tog)***

Pull up a loop in each of next 2 sts, YO and draw through all 3 loops on hook **(counts as one sc)**.

DOUBLE CROCHET 2 TOGETHER ***(abbreviated dc2tog)*** (uses next 2 dc)

★ YO, insert hook in **next** dc, YO and pull up a loop, YO and draw through 2 loops on hook; repeat from ★ once **more**, YO and draw through all 3 loops on hook **(counts as one dc)**.

Ladybug Hat

BODY

With Red, ch 42{45-48}; being careful **not** to twist ch, join with slip st to form a ring.

Rnd 1 (Right side)**:** Ch 3 **(counts as first dc, now and throughout)**, dc in next ch and in each ch around; join with slip st to first dc: 42{45-48} dc.

Note: Loop a short piece of yarn around any stitch to mark Rnd 1 as **right** side.

Rnd 2: Ch 3, turn; dc in next dc changing to Black ***(Fig. 1b, page 35)***, work Cluster in next dc, ★ dc in next 5 dc changing to Black in last dc made, work Cluster in next dc; repeat from ★ around to last 3{6-3} dc, dc in last 3{6-3} dc; join with slip st to first dc: 7{7-8} Clusters and 35{38-40} dc.

Work over Black strands to hide yarn.

Rnd 3: Ch 3, turn; dc in next dc and in each st around; join with slip st to first dc: 42{45-48} dc.

Rnd 4: Ch 3, turn; dc in next 4 dc changing to Black in last dc made, work Cluster in next dc, ★ dc in next 5 dc changing to Black in last dc made, work Cluster in next dc; repeat from ★ around to last 0{3-0} dc ***(see Zeros, page 35)***, dc in last 0{3-0} dc; join with slip st to first dc: 7{7-8} Clusters and 35{38-40} dc.

Rnd 5: Ch 3, turn; dc in next st and in each st around; join with slip st to first dc: 42{45-48} dc.

Size Medium Only - Rnd 6: Ch 3, turn; dc in next dc changing to Black, work Cluster in next dc, ★ dc in next 5 dc changing to Black in last dc made, work Cluster in next dc; repeat from ★ around to last 6 dc, dc in next 4 dc, dc2tog; join with slip st to first dc: 7 Clusters and 37 dc.

Size Large Only - Rnds 6-8: Repeat Rnds 2-4.

SHAPING (All Sizes)

Rnd 1: Ch 1, turn; sc2tog around; join with slip st to first sc: 21{22-24} sc.

Rnd 2: Ch 1, turn; sc in first 1{0-0} sc, sc2tog around; join with slip st to first sc: 11{11-12} sc.

Rnd 3: Ch 1, turn; sc in first 1{1-0} sc, sc2tog around; join with slip st to first sc, finish off leaving a long end for sewing: 6 sc.

Weave yarn end through the sts on Rnd 3 to close ***(Fig. 4, page 35)***; secure yarn.

BRIM

Rnd 1: With **right** side facing and working in free loops of beginning ch ***(Fig. 3, page 35)***, join Black with sc in first ch ***(see Joining With Sc, page 35)***; sc in each ch around; join with slip st to first sc: 42{45-48} sc.

Rnds 2-5: Ch 1, do **not** turn; sc in each sc around; join with slip st to first sc.

Finish off.

Sew novelty button to top of hat.

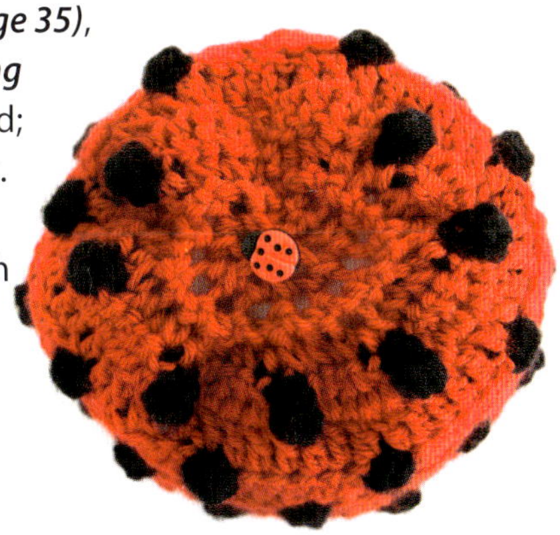

Ladybug Cardigan

Body is worked in one piece to armholes, then divided for the Fronts and Back.

BODY

With Red, ch {63-69}{73-79-85}.

Row 1 (Right side)**:** Dc in fourth ch from hook **(3 skipped chs count as first dc, now and throughout)** and in each ch across: {61-67}{71-77-83} dc.

Note: Loop a short piece of yarn around any stitch to mark Row 1 as **right** side.

Row 2: Ch 3 **(counts as first dc, now and throughout)**, turn; dc in next {2-2}{1-1-1} dc changing to Black in last dc made ***(Fig. 1b, page 35)***, work Cluster in next dc, (dc in next 5 dc changing to Black in last dc made, work Cluster in next dc) across to last {3-3}{2-2-2} dc, dc in last {3-3}{2-2-2} dc: {10-11}{12-13-14} Clusters and {51-56}{59-64-69} dc.

Work over Black strands to hide yarn.

Row 3: Ch 3, turn; dc in next dc and in each st across: {61-67}{71-77-83} dc.

Row 4: Ch 3, turn; dc in next {5-5}{4-4-4} dc changing to Black in last dc made, work Cluster in next dc, (dc in next 5 dc changing to Black in last dc made, work Cluster in next dc) across to last {6-6}{5-5-5} dc, dc in last {6-6}{5-5-5} dc: {9-10}{11-12-13} Clusters and {52-57}{60-65-70} dc.

Row 5: Ch 3, turn; dc in next dc and in each st across: {61-67} {71-77-83} dc.

Working in pattern (Rows 2-5), work {1-1}{3-5-7} row(s).

RIGHT FRONT

Row 1: Ch 3, turn; dc in next {14-15} {16-18-19} sts, leave remaining sts unworked: {15-16}{17-19-20} dc.

Continue to work in pattern throughout, making sure the Clusters line up.

Rows 2 thru {4-5}{5-6-7}: Work across in pattern.

NECK SHAPING

SIZES 6 MONTHS & 3 YEARS ONLY

Row 1: Turn; slip st in first {5}{6} sts, ch 3, dc in next st and in each st across: {11}{14} dc.

Row 2: Ch 3, turn; work across in pattern to last 2 dc, dc2tog: {10}{13} sts.

Row 3: Ch 1, turn; sc in each st across; finish off leaving a long end for sewing.

SIZES 1 YEAR, 2 YEARS, & 4 YEARS ONLY

Row 1: Ch 3, turn; work across in pattern to last {4}{5-5} dc, leave remaining dc unworked: {12}{12-15} sts.

Row 2: Ch 2 **(does not count as a st)**, turn; skip first dc, dc in next st and in each st across: {11}{11-14} dc.

Row 3: Ch 1, turn; sc in each dc across; finish off leaving a long end for sewing.

BACK

Row 1: With **right** side facing, join Red with dc in next unworked st on Body ***(see Joining With Dc, page 35)***; dc in next {30-34}{36-38-42} sts, leave remaining sts unworked: {31-35} {37-39-43} dc.

Rows 2 thru {6-7}{7-8-9}: Work across in pattern.

Last Row: Ch 1, turn; sc in each st across; finish off.

LEFT FRONT

Row 1: With **right** side facing, join Red with dc in next unworked st on Body; dc in next st and in each st across: {15-16}{17-19-20} dc.

Rows 2 thru {4-5}{5-6-7}: Work across in pattern.

NECK SHAPING

SIZES 6 MONTHS & 3 YEARS ONLY

Row 1: Ch 3, turn; dc in next st and in each st across to last {4}{5} sts, leave remaining sts unworked: {11}{14} dc.

Row 2: Ch 2 **(does not count as a st)**, turn; skip first dc, dc in next st, work across: {10}{13} dc.

Row 3: Ch 1, turn; sc in each st across; finish off leaving a long end for sewing.

SIZES 1 YEAR, 2 YEARS, & 4 YEARS ONLY

Row 1: Turn; slip st in first {5}{6-6} sts, ch 3, work across in pattern: {12}{12-15} sts.

Row 2: Ch 3, turn; dc in next st and in each st across to last 2 sts, dc2tog: {11}{11-14} sts.

Row 3: Ch 1, turn; sc in each dc across; finish off leaving a long end for sewing.

SLEEVE (Make 2)

With Red, ch {21-21}{23-23-25}.

Row 1 (Right side)**:** Dc in fourth ch from hook and in each ch across: {19-19}{21-21-23} dc.

Note: Mark Row 1 as **right** side.

Row 2: Ch 3, turn; dc in next {2-2} {3-3-4} dc changing to Black in last dc made, work Cluster in next dc, (dc in next 5 dc changing to Black in last dc made, work Cluster in next dc) twice, dc in last {3-3}{4-4-5} dc: 3 Clusters and {16-16}{18-18-20} dc.

Work over Black strands to hide yarn.

Row 3 (Increase row)**:** Ch 3, turn; dc in first dc and in each st across to last dc, 2 dc in last dc: {21-21} {23-23-25} dc.

Sizes 6 Months & 1 Year Only-
Row 4: Ch 2, drop Red, with Black, ch 1, turn; work Cluster in next dc, (dc in next 5 dc changing to Black in last dc made, work Cluster in next dc) 3 times, dc in last {1-1} dc: 4 Clusters and {17-17} dc.

Sizes 2 Years, 3 Years, & 4 Years Only - Row 4: Ch 3, turn; dc in next {1-1-2} dc changing to Black in last dc made, work Cluster in next dc, (dc in next 5 dc changing to Black in last dc made, work Cluster in next dc) 3 times, dc in last {2-2-3} dc: 4 Clusters and {19-19-21} dc.

All Sizes - Row 5 (Increase row)**:** Ch 3, turn; dc in first dc and in each st across to last dc, 2 dc in last dc: {23-23}{25-25-27} dc.

Working in pattern (Rows 2-5), continue to increase one stitch at each edge, every other row, {0-2}{1-2-3} time(s) **more** ***(see Zeros, page 35)***: {27}{27-29-33} sts.

Work even for {3-1}{5-3-3} row(s).

Last Row: Ch 1, turn; sc in each st across; finish off.

SLEEVE RIBBING

Row 1: With **right** side facing and working in free loops of beginning ch ***(Fig. 3, page 35)***, join Black with dc in first ch; dc in next ch and in each ch across: {19-19}{21-21-23} dc.

Row 2: Ch 2, turn; skip first dc, (work BPdc around next dc, work FPdc around next dc) across; finish off.

FINISHING

With **wrong** sides together, whipstitch shoulder seams ***(Fig. 5a, page 36)***.

Sew Sleeves to armholes, matching center of Sleeves to shoulder seams. Whipstitch underarm seam ***(Fig. 5b, page 36)***.

BOTTOM RIBBING

Row 1: With **right** side facing and working in free loops of beginning ch, join Black with dc in first ch; dc in next ch and in each ch across: {61-67}{71-77-83} dc.

Row 2: Ch 2, turn; skip first dc, (work BPdc around next dc, work FPdc around next dc) across; finish off.

NECK RIBBING

Row 1: With **right** side facing, join Black with dc in first unworked st at Right Front neck edge; dc in next {3-3}{4-4-4} sts, work 7 dc evenly spaced across end of rows, dc in next {11-13}{15-13-15} sc across Back, work 7 dc evenly spaced across end of rows, dc in next {4-4}{5-5-5} sts: {33-35}{39-37-39} dc.

Row 2: Ch 2, turn; skip first dc, (work BPdc around next dc, work FPdc around next dc) across; finish off.

BUTTON BAND

The Button Band is made on the Left Front for Girl's cardigan and on the Right Front for Boy's cardigan.

Row 1: With **right** side facing, join Black with sc in end of first row on Ribbing ***(see Joining With Sc, page 35)***; work {24-24}{29-34-40} sc evenly spaced across Front edge: {25-25}{30-35-41} sc.

Rows 2-5: Ch 1, turn; sc in each sc across.

Finish off.

BUTTONHOLE BAND

Row 1: With **right** side of remaining Front edge facing, join Black with sc in end of first row on Ribbing; work {24-24}{29-34-40} sc evenly spaced across Front edge: {25-25}{30-35-41} sc.

Row 2: Ch 1, turn; sc in each sc across.

Row 3 (Buttonhole row)**:** Ch 1, turn; sc in first 2 sc, ★ ch 1, skip next sc **(buttonhole made)**, sc in next {4-4}{4-4-5} sc; repeat from ★ across to last 3 sc, ch 1, skip next sc, sc in last 2 sc: {5-5}{6-7-7} ch-1 sps.

Row 4: Ch 1, turn; sc in each sc and in each ch-1 sp across: {25-25}{30-35-41} sc.

Row 5: Ch 1, turn; sc in each sc across; finish off.

Sew buttons to Button Band matching buttonholes.

Bumblebee Hat & Cardigan

SHOPPING LIST

Yarn (Medium Weight) 4 MEDIUM

[3.5 ounces, 170 yards (100 grams, 156 meters) per skein]:

- ☐ Black - {1-2}{2-2-2} skein(s)
- ☐ Yellow - {1-1}{1-2-2} skein(s)

Crochet Hook

- ☐ Size J (6 mm) **or** size needed for gauge

Additional Supplies

- ☐ Yarn needle
- ☐ Sewing needle and thread
- ☐ ⅝" (16 mm) Buttons (novelty) - {6-6}{7-8-8}

SIZE INFORMATION

HAT

Size	Finished Circumference	
Small	15¼"	(38.5 cm)
Medium	16¼"	(41.5 cm)
Large	17½"	(44.5 cm)

CARDIGAN

Size	Finished Chest Measurement	
6 months	23¾"	(60.5 cm)
1 year	25¾"	(65.5 cm)
2 years	27¼"	(69 cm)
3 years	29½"	(75 cm)
4 years	31¾"	(80.5 cm)

Size Note: We have printed the instructions for the sizes in different colors to make it easier for you to find:

- Size 6 months & small hat in Blue
- Size 1 year in Pink
- Size 2 years & medium hat in Green
- Size 3 years in Orange
- Size 4 years & large hat in Brown

Instructions in Black apply to all sizes.

GAUGE INFORMATION

11 dc = 4" (10 cm),
4 dc rows = 2½" (6.25 cm)

Gauge Swatch: 4" wide x 2½" high (10 cm x 6.25 cm)

Ch 13.

Row 1: Dc in fourth ch from hook **(3 skipped chs count as first dc)** and in each ch across: 11 dc.

Rows 2-4: Ch 3 **(counts as first dc)**, turn; dc in next dc and in each dc across.

Finish off.

STITCH GUIDE

FRONT POST DOUBLE CROCHET ***(abbreviated FPdc)***

YO, insert hook from **front** to **back** around post of st indicated ***(Fig. 2, page 35)***, YO and pull up a loop (3 loops on hook), (YO and draw through 2 loops on hook) twice.

BACK POST DOUBLE CROCHET ***(abbreviated BPdc)***

YO, insert hook from **back** to **front** around post of st indicated ***(Fig. 2, page 35)***, YO and pull up a loop (3 loops on hook), (YO and draw through 2 loops on hook) twice.

SINGLE CROCHET 2 TOGETHER ***(abbreviated sc2tog)***

Pull up a loop in each of next 2 sts, YO and draw through all 3 loops on hook **(counts as one sc)**.

DOUBLE CROCHET 2 TOGETHER ***(abbreviated dc2tog)*** (uses next 2 dc)

★ YO, insert hook in **next** dc, YO and pull up a loop, YO and draw through 2 loops on hook; repeat from ★ once **more**, YO and draw through all 3 loops on hook **(counts as one dc)**.

Bumblebee Hat

BODY

With Yellow, ch 42{45-48}; being careful **not** to twist ch, join with slip st to form a ring.

Rnd 1 (Right side)**:** Ch 3 **(counts as first dc, now and throughout)**, dc in next ch and in each ch around; join with slip st to first dc: 42{45-48} dc.

Note: Loop a short piece of yarn around any stitch to mark Rnd 1 as **right** side.

Rnd 2: Ch 3, turn; dc in next dc and in each dc around; drop Yellow, with Black, join with slip st to first dc ***(Fig. 1c, page 35)***.

Carry unused yarn on **wrong** side.

Rnd 3: Ch 3, turn; dc in next dc and in each dc around; join with slip st to first dc.

Rnd 4: Ch 3, turn; dc in next dc and in each dc around; drop yarn, with previous color, join with slip st to first dc.

Rnds 5 and 6: Repeat Rnds 3 and 4.

SIZE SMALL ONLY

Rnd 7: Ch 1, turn; sc in each dc around; join with slip st to first sc.

Rnd 8: Ch 1, turn; sc2tog around; cut Yellow, with Black, join with slip st to first sc: 21 sc.

Rnds 9 and 10: Ch 1, turn; sc in first sc, sc2tog around; join with slip st to first sc, finish off leaving a long end for sewing: 6 sc.

SIZE MEDIUM ONLY

Rnd 7: Ch 3, turn; dc2tog around; join with slip st to first dc: 23 dc.

Rnd 8: Ch 3, turn; dc2tog around; cut Black, with Yellow, join with slip st to first dc: 12 dc.

Rnd 9: Ch 1, turn; sc2tog around; join with slip st to first sc, finish off leaving a long end for sewing: 6 sc.

SIZE LARGE ONLY

Rnd 7: Repeat Rnd 3.

Rnd 8: Repeat Rnd 4; cut Black.

Rnds 9-11: Ch 1, turn; sc2tog around; join with slip st to first sc, finish off leaving a long end for sewing: 6 sc.

ALL SIZES

Weave yarn end through the sts on last rnd to close ***(Fig. 4, page 35)***; secure yarn.

BRIM

Rnd 1: With **right** side facing and working in free loops of beginning ch ***(Fig. 3, page 35)***, join Black with dc in first ch ***(see Joining With Dc, page 35)***, dc in next ch and in each ch around to last 0{1-0} ch(s) ***(see Zeros, page 35)***, skip last 0{1-0} ch(s); join with slip st to first dc: 42{44-48} dc.

Rnd 2: Ch 2, turn; work FPdc around next dc, (work BPdc around next dc, work FPdc around next dc) around; join with slip st to first st, finish off.

Sew novelty button to top of hat.

Bumblebee Cardigan

Body is worked in one piece to armholes, then divided for the Fronts and Back.

BODY

With Yellow, ch {63-69}{73-79-85}.

Row 1 (Right side)**:** Dc in fourth ch from hook (**3 skipped chs count as first dc, now and throughout**) and in each ch across: {61-67}{71-77-83} dc.

Note: Loop a short piece of yarn around any stitch to mark Row 1 as **right** side.

Row 2: Ch 3 (**counts as first dc, now and throughout**), turn; dc in next dc and in each dc across changing to Black in last dc *(Fig. 1b, page 35)*.

Carry unused yarn along edge.

Row 3: Ch 3, turn; dc in next dc and in each dc across.

Next {3-3}{5-7-9} Rows: Repeat Row 3 for pattern, changing colors every other row.

RIGHT FRONT

Row 1: Ch 3, turn; dc in next {14-15}{16-18-19} dc, leave remaining dc unworked: {15-16}{17-19-20} dc.

Continue to change colors every other row throughout.

Rows 2 thru {4-5}{5-6-7}: Ch 3, turn; dc in next dc and in each dc across.

NECK SHAPING

SIZES 6 MONTHS & 3 YEARS ONLY

Row 1: Turn; slip st in first {5}{6} dc, ch 3, dc in next dc and in each dc across: {11}{14} dc.

Row 2: Ch 3, turn; dc in next dc and in each dc across to last 2 dc, dc2tog; finish off leaving a long end for sewing: {10}{13} dc.

SIZES 1 YEAR, 2 YEARS, & 4 YEARS ONLY

Row 1: Ch 3, turn; dc in next dc and in each dc across to last {4}{5-5} dc, leave remaining dc unworked: {12}{12-15} dc.

Row 2: Ch 2 **(does not count as a st)**, turn; skip first dc, dc in next dc and in each dc across; finish off leaving a long end for sewing: {11}{11-14} dc.

BACK

Row 1: With **right** side facing, join next color with dc in next unworked dc on Body ***(see Joining With Dc, page 35)***; dc in next {30-34}{36-38-42} dc, leave remaining dc unworked: {31-35}{37-39-43} dc.

Rows 2 thru {6-7}{7-8-9}: Ch 3, turn; dc in next dc and in each dc across.

Finish off.

LEFT FRONT

Row 1: With **right** side facing, join next color with dc in next unworked dc on Body; dc in next dc and in each dc across: {15-16}{17-19-20} dc.

Rows 2 thru {4-5}{5-6-7}: Ch 3, turn; dc in next dc and in each dc across.

NECK SHAPING

SIZES 6 MONTHS & 3 YEARS ONLY

Row 1: Ch 3, turn; dc in next dc and in each dc across to last {4}{5} dc, leave remaining dc unworked: {11}{14} dc.

Row 2: Ch 2 **(does not count as a st)**, turn; skip first dc, dc in next dc and in each dc across; finish off leaving a long end for sewing: {10}{13} dc.

SIZES 1 YEAR, 2 YEARS, & 4 YEARS ONLY

Row 1: Turn; slip st in first {5}{6-6} dc, ch 3, dc in next dc and in each dc across: {12}{12-15} dc.

Row 2: Ch 3, turn; dc in next dc and in each dc across to last 2 dc, dc2tog; finish off leaving a long end for sewing: {11}{11-14} dc.

SLEEVE (Make 2)

With Yellow, ch {21-21}{23-23-25}.

Row 1 (Right side)**:** Dc in fourth ch from hook and in each ch across: {19-19}{21-21-23} dc.

Note: Mark Row 1 as **right** side.

Row 2: Ch 3, turn; dc in next dc and in each dc across changing to Black in last dc.

Carry unused yarn along edge.

Row 3 (Increase row)**:** Ch 3, turn; dc in first dc and in each dc across to last dc, 2 dc in last dc: {21-21}{23-23-25} dc.

Row 4: Ch 3, turn; dc in next dc and in each dc across changing colors in last dc.

Repeat Rows 3 and 4, {1-3}{2-3-4} time(s): {23-27}{27-29-33} dc.

Work even for {2-0}{4-2-2} rows ***(see Zeros, page 35)***.

Finish off.

SLEEVE RIBBING

Row 1: With **right** side facing and working in free loops of beginning ch ***(Fig. 3, page 35)***, join Black with dc in first ch; dc in next ch and in each ch across: {19-19}{21-21-23} dc.

Row 2: Ch 2, turn; skip first dc, (work BPdc around next dc, work FPdc around next dc) across; finish off.

FINISHING

With **wrong** sides together, whipstitch shoulder seams ***(Fig. 5a, page 36)***.

Sew Sleeves to armholes, matching center of Sleeves to shoulder seams. Whipstitch underarm seam ***(Fig. 5b, page 36)***.

BOTTOM RIBBING

Row 1: With **right** side facing and working in free loops of beginning ch, join Black with dc in first ch; dc in next ch and in each ch across: {61-67}{71-77-83} dc.

Row 2: Ch 2, turn; skip first dc, (work BPdc around next dc, work FPdc around next dc) across; finish off.

NECK RIBBING

Row 1: With **right** side facing, join Black with dc in first unworked st at Right Front neck edge; dc in next {3-3}{4-4-4} sts, work 7 dc evenly spaced across end of rows, dc in next {11-13}{15-13-15} sc across Back, work 7 dc evenly spaced across end of rows, dc in next {4-4}{5-5-5} sts: {33-35}{39-37-39} dc.

Row 2: Ch 2, turn; skip first dc, (work BPdc around next dc, work FPdc around next dc) across; finish off.

BUTTON BAND

The Button Band is made on the Left Front for Girl's cardigan and on the Right Front for Boy's cardigan.

Row 1: With **right** side facing, join Black with sc in end of first row on Ribbing ***(see Joining With Sc, page 35)***; work {24-24}{29-34-40} sc evenly spaced across Front edge: {25-25}{30-35-41} sc.

Rows 2-5: Ch 1, turn; sc in each sc across.

Finish off.

BUTTONHOLE BAND

Row 1: With **right** side of remaining Front edge facing, join Black with sc in end of first row on Ribbing; work {24-24}{29-34-40} sc evenly spaced across Front edge: {25-25}{30-35-41} sc.

Row 2: Ch 1, turn; sc in each sc across.

Row 3 (Buttonhole row)**:** Ch 1, turn; sc in first 2 sc, ★ ch 1, skip next sc **(buttonhole made)**, sc in next {4-4}{4-4-5} sc; repeat from ★ across to last 3 sc, ch 1, skip next sc, sc in last 2 sc: {5-5}{6-7-7} ch-1 sps.

Row 4: Ch 1, turn; sc in each sc and in each ch-1 sp across: {25-25}{30-35-41} sc.

Row 5: Ch 1, turn; sc in each sc across; finish off.

Sew buttons to Button Band matching buttonholes.

General Instructions

ABBREVIATIONS

BPdc	Back Post double crochet(s)
ch(s)	chain(s)
cm	centimeters
dc	double crochet(s)
dc2tog	double crochet 2 together
dtr	double treble crochet(s)
FPdc	Front Post double crochet(s)
hdc	half double crochet(s)
mm	millimeters
Rnd(s)	Round(s)
sc	single crochet(s)
sc2tog	single crochet 2 together
sp(s)	space(s)
st(s)	stitch(es)
tr	treble crochet(s)
YO	yarn over

SYMBOLS & TERMS

★ — work instructions following ★ as many **more** times as indicated in addition to the first time.

† to † — work all instructions from first † to second † **as many** times as specified.

( ) or [ ] — work enclosed instructions **as many** times as specified by the number immediately following **or** work all enclosed instructions in the stitch or space indicated **or** contains explanatory remarks.

colon (:) — the number(s) given after a colon at the end of a row or round denote(s) the number of stitches or spaces you should have on that row or round.

work even — work without increasing or decreasing in the established pattern.

CROCHET TERMINOLOGY		
UNITED STATES		INTERNATIONAL
slip stitch (slip st)	=	single crochet (sc)
single crochet (sc)	=	double crochet (dc)
half double crochet (hdc)	=	half treble crochet (htr)
double crochet (dc)	=	treble crochet (tr)
treble crochet (tr)	=	double treble crochet (dtr)
double treble crochet (dtr)	=	triple treble crochet (ttr)
triple treble crochet (tr tr)	=	quadruple treble crochet (qtr)
skip	=	miss

Yarn Weight Symbol & Names	LACE 0	SUPER FINE 1	FINE 2	LIGHT 3	MEDIUM 4	BULKY 5	SUPER BULKY 6	JUMBO 7
Type of Yarns in Category	Fingering, size 10 crochet thread	Sock, Fingering, Baby	Sport, Baby	DK, Light Worsted	Worsted, Afghan, Aran	Chunky, Craft, Rug	Super Bulky, Roving	Jumbo, Roving
Crochet Gauge* Ranges in Single Crochet to 4" (10 cm)	32-42 sts**	21-32 sts	16-20 sts	12-17 sts	11-14 sts	8-11 sts	6-9 sts	5 sts and fewer
Advised Hook Size Range	Steel*** 6 to 8, Regular hook B-1	B-1 to E-4	E-4 to 7	7 to I-9	I-9 to K-10½	K-10½ to M/N-13	M/N-13 to Q	Q and larger

*GUIDELINES ONLY: The chart above reflects the most commonly used gauges and hook sizes for specific yarn categories.

** Lace weight yarns are usually crocheted with larger hooks to create lacy openwork patterns. Accordingly, a gauge range is difficult to determine. Always follow the gauge stated in your pattern.

*** Steel crochet hooks are sized differently from regular hooks–the higher the number, the smaller the hook, which is the reverse of regular hook sizing.

CROCHET HOOKS																	
U.S.	B-1	C-2	D-3	E-4	F-5	G-6	7	H-8	I-9	J-10	K-10½	L-11	M/N-13	N/P-15	P/Q	Q	S
Metric - mm	2.25	2.75	3.25	3.5	3.75	4	4.5	5	5.5	6	6.5	8	9	10	15	16	19

■□□□ **BEGINNER**	Projects for first-time crocheters using basic stitches. Minimal shaping.
■■□□ **EASY**	Projects using yarn with basic stitches, repetitive stitch patterns, simple color changes, and simple shaping and finishing.
■■■□ **INTERMEDIATE**	Projects using a variety of techniques, such as basic lace patterns or color patterns, mid-level shaping and finishing.
■■■■ **EXPERIENCED**	Projects with intricate stitch patterns, techniques and dimension, such as non-repeating patterns, multi-color techniques, fine threads, small hooks, detailed shaping and refined finishing.

GAUGE

Exact gauge is **essential** for proper size or fit. Before beginning your project, make the sample swatch given in the individual instructions in the yarn and hook specified. After completing the swatch, measure it, counting your stitches and rows carefully. If your swatch is larger or smaller than specified, **make another, changing hook size to get the correct gauge**. Keep trying until you find the size hook that will give you the specified gauge.

ZEROS

To consolidate the length of an involved pattern, zeros are sometimes used so that all sizes can be combined. For example, sc2tog around to last 0{1-0} sc, sc in last 0{1-0} sc, means the first and last sizes would sc2tog around to the beginning and the medium size would sc in the last sc.

JOINING WITH SC

When instructed to join with sc, begin with a slip knot on hook. Insert hook in stitch or space indicated, YO and pull up a loop, YO and draw through both loops on hook.

JOINING WITH DC

When instructed to join with dc, begin with a slip knot on hook. YO, holding loop on hook, insert hook in stitch or space indicated, YO and pull up a loop (3 loops on hook), (YO and draw through 2 loops on hook) twice.

CHANGING COLORS

To change colors while working a stitch, work the stitch to within one step of completion, drop yarn, hook new yarn ***(Figs. 1a & b)*** and draw through both loops on hook. Do **not** cut yarn until indicated.

Fig. 1a

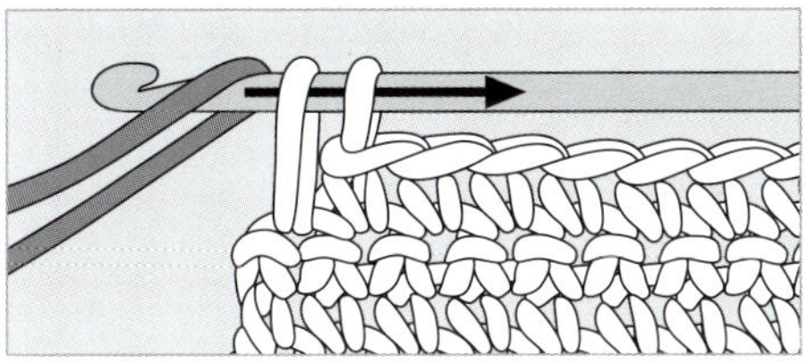

Fig. 1b

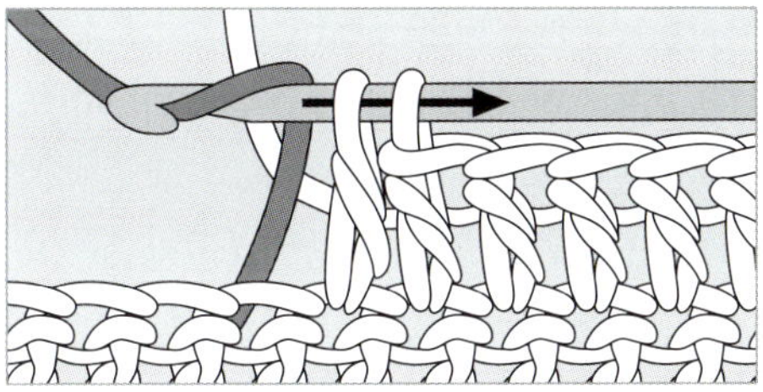

To change colors while joining with a slip st, drop yarn, insert hook in first stitch, hook new yarn and draw through st and loop on hook *(Fig. 1c)*.

Fig. 1c

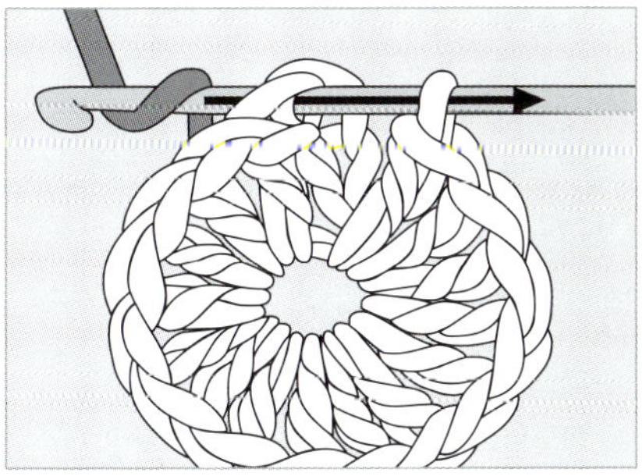

POST STITCH

Work around post of stitch indicated, inserting hook in direction of arrow *(Fig. 2)*.

Fig. 2

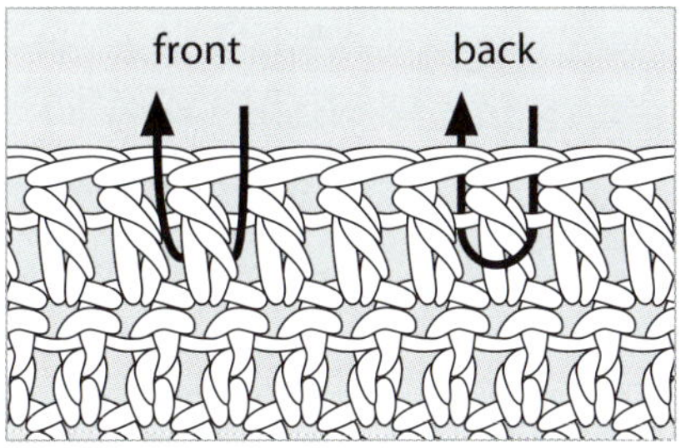

FREE LOOPS OF CHAIN

When instructed to work in free loops of a chain, work in loop indicated by arrow *(Fig. 3)*.

Fig. 3

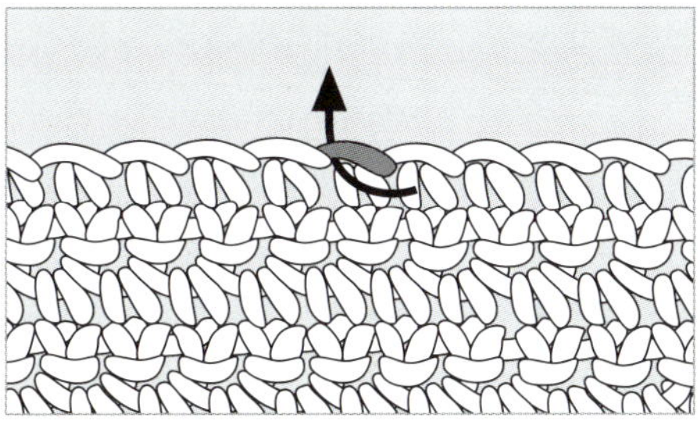

WEAVING THRU STITCHES

Weave yarn end through the stitches *(Fig. 4)* and gather to close.

Fig. 4

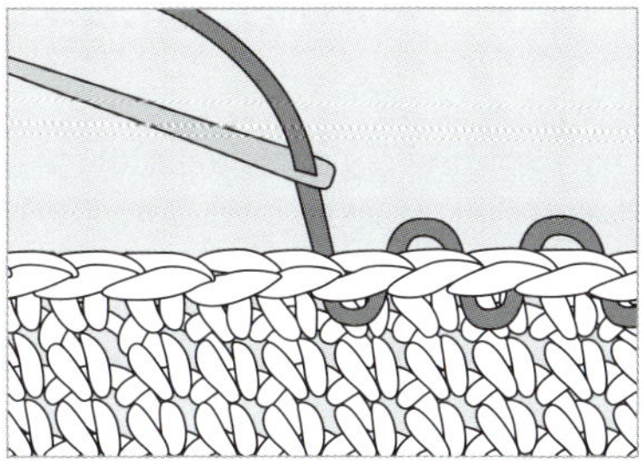

WHIPSTITCH

With **wrong** sides together, sew through both pieces once to secure the beginning of the seam, leaving an ample yarn end to weave in later. Insert the needle from **right** to **left** through two strands on each piece ***(Fig. 5a)* or** through end of rows ***(Fig. 5b)***. Bring the needle around and insert it from **right** to **left** through the next strand on both pieces.
Repeat along the edge, being careful to match stitches or rows.

Fig. 5a

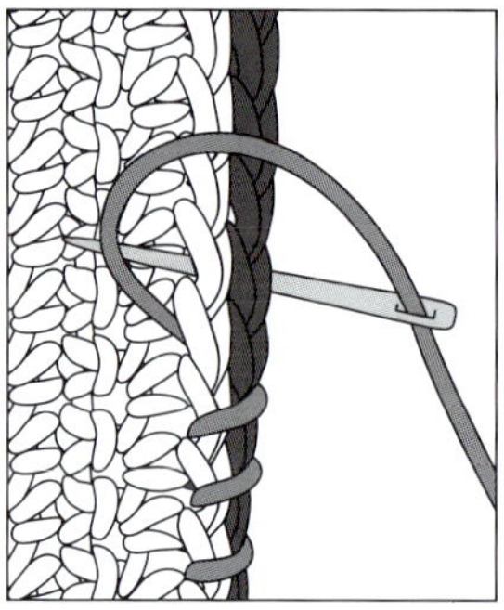

Fig. 5b

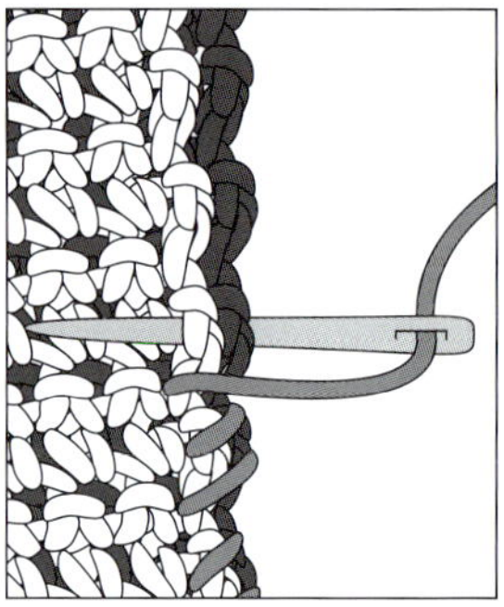

Yarn Information

The items in this book were made using a medium weight yarn. Any brand of medium weight yarn may be used. It is best to refer to the yardage/meters when determining how many balls or skeins to purchase. Remember, to arrive at the finished size, it is the GAUGE/TENSION that is important, not the brand of yarn.

For your convenience, listed below are the yarns used to create our photography models. Because yarn manufacturers make frequent changes in their product lines, you may sometimes find it necessary to use a substitute yarn or to search for the discontinued product at alternate suppliers (locally or online).

BUTTERFLIES SET

Lion Brand® Vanna's Choice®
Main Color (Blue) - #111 Sky Blue
Contrasting Color (Purple) - #146 Dusty Purple
Color A (Dark Blue) - #183 Periwinkle
Color B (Aqua) - #106 Aquamarine
Color C (Lilac) - #191 Lilac
Color D (Pink) - #104 Pink Grapefruit
Color E (Green) - #175 Radiant Lime

STAR-STRUCK SET

Lion Brand® Vanna's Choice®
Black - #153 Black
Navy - #110 Navy
Blue - #105 Silver Blue
Dark Grey - #151 Charcoal Grey

Lion Brand® Vanna's Complement
Grey - #405 Silver Heather

LADYBUG & BUMBLEBEE SET

Lion Brand® Vanna's Choice®
Black - #153 Black
Red - #113 Scarlet
Yellow - #158 Mustard

We have made every effort to ensure that these instructions are accurate and complete. We cannot, however, be responsible for human error, typographical mistakes, or variations in individual work.

Production Team: Instructional/Technical Editor - Cathy Hardy; Editorial Writer - Susan Frantz Wiles; Senior Graphic Artist - Lora Puls; Graphic Artist - Kellie McAnulty; Photo Stylist - Stephanie Moore; and Photographer - Jason Masters.